Dazzle Ship

DAZZLE SHIP

ISABEL GALLEYMORE

worple press

First published in 2014 by
Worple Press
Achill Sound, 2b Dry Hill Road
Tonbridge
Kent TN9 1LX.
www.worplepress.co.uk

Cover image, "Study of Ships with Five Colors", by Abbott
Handerson Thayer, ca. 1910. Watercolor on paper. 11½ x 8¾ in.
Image courtesy of the Family and Estate of Abbott Handerson Thayer.
Digitally altered and manipulated from the original image.

Printed by imprintdigital
Upton Pyne, Exeter
www.imprintdigital.net

Typeset by narrator
www.narrator.me.uk
info@narrator.me.uk
033 022 300 39

ISBN: 978-1-905208-28-9

Acknowledgements

Thanks are due to the editors of *Poetry London*, *Poetry Review*, *Entanglements: New Ecopoetry* and *The Arts of Peace* where some of these poems first appeared.

I am also grateful to Dr Andy Brown, Robert Peake, Peter Carpenter, Michael Rose-Steel and to all those involved with the Aldeburgh Eight 2013.

Contents

A Castle or a Folly

It could be at a party —
a response leaves you standing
like you're looking towards a crest
where someone's built what could be
a castle or a folly.
The tone of voice, the choice of words,
the ambiguous intent behind
each stone that forms the battlement.
For all you know the keep is full
of watermelons; as they swell
they creak like arrows
pulled against bows.

Petal & Stream

When I say a petal is like a stream
this is a match-maker's introduction
rousing a chemistry.

The stream considers how to belong
to the colour, the blooming, the bees;
the petal tries on the stream's surname,
a life of rushing transparency.

Neither can see how this will work
till one touches the other's soft face
and instantly both agree.

Forest

One thing is liked by another:

snake and creeper,
leaf and green frog –

they try to complete
each other's sentences.

It shouldn't go further
than this flirt and rumour:

the sloth who takes her own limb
for an algae-furred branch

drops through the tangle
of the forest canopy

holding only onto herself.

The Smallholding

When he weeded or dug the beds
to sow swiss chard or turnip seeds
or painted or fixed the whitewood fence,
fruit would fall with small hushed thuds.
Hearing each drop he could've said
its name – whether Gala or Cox –
how sweet or green it was, and when
his wife's foot lands into the house
after her morning trip into town
from heel against the stone he'll know
whether the heels of an army will follow.

Uprising

Consider how this dandelion
is a microphone of seeds
set above a silent crowd

awaiting just one utterance
to transmit a hundred
smaller scaffoldings

of a thought or an idea
or a dream that soon will wake
from the ground with torches lit.

Notes on Death as the Other Woman

Sue takes the musical score from his desk.
He's serving four months on a dazzle ship.
The sun trips into the mirror – and by the light
of this small explosion she finds its cover
holds the ghost of his last note.
Fragments move as if he's still writing,
certain scrawled words become Chinese whispers:
Dear / Death [...] *the life I lead / I leave* [...]
Under that black dress I sucked your breasts.

The score drops the length of Sue's floral pinafore.
She takes the bin out. Castor and Pollux
are lit in the sky. There's a man up the road
but she can't say whether he's walking
towards her or walking away.

Sweet Peas

When the fiddle
starts up
in the throat
of the sparrow
they will take
their places
and bow to their
partners, skip
four paces, hop left
turn right
and repeat until
the pairs reunite –
they'll soon appear
enwoven
with each other –
yet Love doesn't
train them,
they lead their lives
as we do, mindful
of climbing
various ladders:
her hand
holds his face –
there she finds
a new footing

Bond

What can be said of the bond between sea anemone and crab?
The sting of the first defends the other and, in return,
the pincers feed the squat jelly-mouth. Is this so unlike the clerk
and housewife? She wears a pink apron and prepares fish dinners
to keep his embrace. And what can be said of this metaphor – is
the symbiosis between image and matter as mutual as that
under the water? Or does it suck the roar out of nature as when man
claims he's a lion, a tiger?

Girl & Father

This girl sitting on her father's shoulders
is and is not her father:

they are one small giant
with four arms two stacked heads,

they are simply two different people together.

Two different people,
but one is carrying another –

one carries the form of the eyes,
the contempt for pineapple
and the walk that prioritizes toe over heel
years after they disassemble.

Wren

And the wren barely has wings
she's all drop and drawing into the leaves
she's a body tagged onto a beak

and the girl drawn into a kiss
drops her arms like they're luggage
to become a body tagging onto a beak

and without thinking first
she sings about this birdily
tagged to the world by her beak

Replacings

The way a heart isn't
because today it is a bird.
How much offered, how much withdrawn
by wings & migratory instinct.
The way a bird isn't
because today it is a heart.
How much offered, how much withdrawn
by keeping pace & devotional instinct.

My head upon a pillow
where your hand would rest.
How much offered, how much withdrawn
by what my head already holds.
The way my legs aren't
because yours are so outstretched.
What offered, what withdrawn
by these, atwitch with your dream.

from **The Schmees**

Not *pumpkin*, not *sunshine*, not *baby*.
They were to christen themselves differently.
In an April cloudy with blossom
they drink Les Gémeaux in the garden.
He takes off her name like a dress.

Who said *schmee* first? It doesn't matter –
they both speak the word to wake one another
to the world they're collaging piece by piece.
Last week it rushed from her mouth on the street
and an old man turned with a curve in his spine
expecting the smallness of children.

Where does the word come from?
Maybe it's the sound of a smile, schmee says
see – schmee – and all his teeth show.

On Fullness

When something's brimming isn't it closed?

After a night of rain
the bowl outside is sealed with water –

I'm picturing small houses
holding parties, I'm picturing hearts

to consider what can't gain admittance
when what is full is empty of space –

inside a notebook thickened with ink
words overlap, lose sense,
paper can no longer hear itself think.

Together

the heart aflame no longer
shines any light on love
because they are always together –

because they are always together
it's hard to see them apart
like the blade in the blade of grass –

two lovers grew so close they became
too fluently familiar
having lost what makes fire fire

Cycle

after Francis Ponge's 'Le Cycle des Saisons'

A bud comes forth from the throat
and stuffs the mouth with an expression:
a dandelion head about to burst open,
a leaf furled like a new shaving brush.

The buds think they say everything afresh.

By the same unfolding and bright yellow gesture
they only say *leaf*, they only say *flower*.

Believing they've failed to make themselves heard
they grow taller and bigger and so lose their form.

They tire. The mouth that opened for them
dries up. That which was said, so eagerly,
now discolours, withers and drops.

Harvest

After stripping the branches of berries
the robin held a handful of seeds
in her stomach: the robin carried a tree
– in fact she secretly sowed a whole forest –
a store of bows and arrows and shields.
Years found the bird had planted a battle,
her tiny body had borne the new king.

Men looked up to the skies and blessed
or blamed the planets moving overhead.
A blackbird, meanwhile, started to pick
at the fruit both armies had left.

A Toad

Because of its size and lurch
a toad is likened to a man's heart – but
what happens to the heart of the toad

that's bean-shaped yet intricate
where wants write into the muscle
as water sculpts stone?

Does it become vestigial –
irrelevant within this human frame
or can the toad's heart keep

like the conch shell trumpet
blown, but filling again
with its own sea-sound.

The Crab

Sunbathing on basalt,
the crab is a miniature
cedarwood stage
moving upon pincers
and ginger-haired legs –
empty of actors,
this stage casually
bears a backdrop;
a skywash of sea,
a suggestion of birds,
how its scale frames
an old local story
with these barnacles
empty, ashen
as blown volcanoes.

Dartmoor Tinners

Candlesticks, organ pipes, bells
came downriver in fits and starts.
The tailings, the what–isn't–tin,
we threw back in – silting the ports

so the ships were built smaller
and yet still hauled what would become
the sound of a bronzy Venetian Mass,
some buttons, some cups.

Now we unwrap the moor
and burrow deeper than the long-ears
to raise Wheal Jane, Wheal Prosper:

we'll be drawing out the idea of a lamp
that won't surface for two-hundred years
when, among our singing, the candle's first
to realise the bad air and black out.

A Rose

has folded itself so it can unfold,
has put on a haematine colour,
put on a little weight
so you'll call it a human heart –
and presuming this an invitation
the rose climbs in behind your sternum.

Everywhere, roses are doing this now.

The roses steal fragments of conversations
we barely realise we have with ourselves
tapping the calls from various hurts
to restyle their wooden claws.

Cracked Walnut and Cup

The cracked walnut
beside the porcelain cup

is not a porcelain walnut
and a cracked cup

but as she who finds
her lover's words in her mouth

and their friends who discover
their faces alike

the walnut shell seems
another drinking vessel

and the cup appears
ever more breakable.

I'm doing you an injustice

It's like I've invited you to a party
of people I know but you don't –
I see you fitting into the erratic
spaces between people talking
till I only see parts of you
like the nude beneath the willow
she doesn't look quite herself
dappled by the shadowings
from what is given light first.

Barnacle

Barnacle, the author's intention, wears
a little ivory hat. In the sea-dark he captains
a solid idea from the depths.
Other intentions cluster:
a kind of rugby scrum occurs,
and while they argue back and forth
about what the ball represents
the rock they cover begins to move
like a wave with a life of its own.
Barnacle & friends become hitchhikers
but not one will notice until
they reach waters of knifejaw and gemfish
or beach upon a blank coast.

Holy Well

*Legend tells that the well contained 3 fish, and
as long as St Neot ate no more than one fish a
day their number would never decrease.*

Those seeking health, those whose
cells do not divide quickly enough,
visit this small installation of blessed
multiplications an angel once promised
– *two fish will be three fish by the next
day, and always, as long as you only eat
one.* There are no fish now – but where
there's water there's a whether of matter
– see how the coins someone's placed in
the ripple are becoming uncertain of their
solid circles, copying their colour onto
the granite floor until this well fills with
thoughts of halos.

Wishbone

After Arthur Ganson

A wishbone walked across the city
harnessed to a delicate mechanism
of cogs & pulleys,
springs & wheels
made from wire as thin as thought.

Past a broken-down bus,
the feet of drunks outside the Three Bells
and a dog with its focused, salivating mouth,
this fine technology of hope pushed
to keep the wishbone swaggering
like a tiny cowboy made from the moon.